Linux

The Beginner's Crash Course

TOM WELLING

within this document, including, but not limited to, —errors, omissions, or inaccuracies.

Contents

Introduction

Thank you for downloading "Linux: The Beginner's Crash Course." Linux is one of the most used operating systems in the world. This book is a beginner's guide to understanding the potential of Linux and how to use it to perform the basic tasks.

I have done my best to ensure that you can get a good overview of the various advantages of this OS and things you need to be careful of. Most of the contents of this book are derived from the practical use of Linux as well as multiple reference sources for various types of the Linux commands.

The book will educate you on multiple aspects of the Linux OS and its application. I sincerely hope you can use the information as a stepping stone before you begin your in-depth learning on the subject.

Chapter 1: Understanding Linux

Linux is an operating system, just like MAC OS X, Windows 8 and Windows 10. It is software that manages all of the hardware resources related to the desktop or laptop. Do you know what exactly Linux does? In simple words, it is the operating system that is the bridge between your system software and the hardware. The operating system plays a very important part in keeping the unit working and your software functioning.

Why Linux? How is it Different from Other Operating Systems?

Linux, a fast and stable open source OS for personal computers (PCs) and workstations, features professional-level online services, a wide array of development tools and fully functional graphical user interfaces (GUIs). Applications ranging from simple office suites to complex multimedia are also featured by Linux. Linus Torvalds developed Linux in the early 1990s in collaboration with other distinguished programmers of the time around the globe. The functions performed by Linux as an operating system are pretty much similar to that performed by other operations systems like Windows, Macintosh, Unix and Windows NT. Linux stands out from rest due to its free availability, power, and adaptability. Almost all PC operating were developed within the confines of small PCs, and their functioning was limited to restricted PCs. They have become versatile only recently with the up gradation. Upgrading is constantly needed for these operating systems due to the ever-changing capabilities of the PC hardware. Linux was developed under different circumstances. It is a PC version of the Unix operating system. Unix has been used on mainframes and minicomputers and now used by network servers and workstations. Linux has brought the speed, flexibility, efficiency and measurability of Unix to your PC through maximum use of PCs capabilities.

Linux provides GUIs, along with GNOME and KDE, with the same flexibility and power. With Windows and Mac, you don't get the freedom to choose your interface. Linux not only lets you have that freedom, but you can further customize the interface. You can add panels, applications, desktops and menus. You get all the Internet-aware tools and drag and drop capabilities along with these additions.

Historical Context

Unix operating system was developed in a special context and to completely understand and appreciate Linux, you should understand the basics of Unix operating system. Unix was developed in an academic and research environment, unlike other operating systems. The system mostly used in research laboratories, universities, data centers and enterprises is Unix. The computer and communication revolution has paralleled with the development of Unix over the past decades. New computer technologies were developed by computer professionals on Unix, like the ones made for the Internet. The Unix system is no doubt sophisticated, but it is made to be flexible right from the beginning. Different versions can be made for Unix after slight or substantial modifications. It is interesting to note that many different vendors have different versions of official Unix. IBM, Hewlett-Packard and Sun are some examples which sell and maintain their own versions of Unix. The peculiarity and special needs of a particular research program require Unix to be tweaked and tailored in conformity with those demands. The flexibility of Unix doesn't affect the quality, in any way whatsoever. On the contrary, it proves the adaptability of the system which can be molded according to the situation and needs. So Linux was developed in this context with the great adaptability of its predecessor (if we may call it that). Linux is, in fact, a special version of Unix made for PC. Linux is developed in the same way Unix was designed, by the computer professional rendering their service in research like environment. Linux is free and publicly licensed. This shows the deep sense of public service and support which Unix has as it was developed in academic institutions. Linus is accessible to everyone (free of cost), and it is a top rated operating system with its popularity only destined to increase in coming times.

How Linux operates?

Linux is basically divided into three main components: the kernel, the environment, and file structure. The kernel is the main program, controlling and managing the hardware devices like the printer. The environment gives the user with the interface. Commands are received by the environment and transmitted as instructions to the kernel for execution. The way files are stored on the storage system is organized by the file structure. Files are saved and organized in the form of directories. A directory may hold subdirectories, each containing many files. The basic structure of Linux operating system is formed by these three constituents. You can operate the system by interacting and managing files. We will have a look at them separately to form an understanding of how they work.

The operating system has many parts that make it function successfully, and the list of important ones is mentioned below:

The Kernel

It is known to be one of the most important parts of the operating system. No operating system can function properly without this piece. It is the core of the operating system and controls the entire Central Processing Unit. This part has control over the processes occurring in the OS. It is known to be the first element that the system is loaded with, without this, you cannot move forward to the next step. Microkernels were initially used, and they encompassed only the CPU, memory, and IPC. Linux, on the other hand, is a monolithic kernel. It also encompasses the device drivers, file system management, and server system calls. Monolithic kernels are more accessible to hardware and good at multitasking because it can directly access information from the memory or other processes and doesn't have to wait. The Kernel manages the remainder of the system. This part is also responsible for running memory as well as communicating with peripherals such as speakers and others.

The Bootloader

As the name indicates, it is the software that controls the boot procedures of the laptop or computer. Many users would have noticed this as a splash screen popping up and then going away to the boot in an operating system.

With Linux, you get the ability to shift between different versions of Linux kernel or other operating systems you might have installed on your system. A boot management utility, the Grand Unified

Bootloader (GRUB) is responsible for selecting and starting a particular operating system or kernel. It is a versatile management tool which not only lets you load different operating systems but also gives you the choice to choose from different kernels installed, and all of this on a single Linux system.

The Environment

The kernel and user interact through an interface provided by an environment. This interface acts as an interpreter. Commands which are entered by the users are interpreted by the interface and sent to the kernel. There are different kinds of environments, namely, desktop, window managers, and command line shells. A user can set his or her user interface. The environments can be altered by the users according to their special needs, regardless of the kind of environment they opt. The operating system works as an operating environment for the user, in this respect which can be controlled by the user. It is known to be among one of the most creative and interesting programs. It is a puzzle that the users interact with. This program is also one of the most interactive pieces of the operating system. The system has a number of desktop environments to select from according to their preferences, such as Cinnamon, KDE, Enlightenment, XFCE, Unity, etc. Every desktop environment has a number of built-in applications like web browsers, games, tools, configurations and more.

The environment plays a vital part in the working of Linux. We will have a look at two most popular environments in order to understand what they entail.

GNOME

GNOME also known as GNU Network Object Model Environment is powerful, and most popular Linux desktop environment. It can be easily managed by the user, and especially if you are a beginner. It consists primarily of a desktop, a panel, and a set of graphical interface tools with the help of program interfaces are usually constructed. GNOME is designed in such a way that it can provide a flexible platform for the development of exciting and powerful applications. Almost every distribution support GNOME while Red Hat and Fedora serve it as their primary interface. GNU Public

License deals with its release, and it is free of cost. The source code, documentations, and other GNOME software can be easily downloaded from their website at gnome.org

Most Ubuntu distribution users are familiar with GNOME. The reason for its popular lies in the fact that it is easy to use, and also because it is fairly low on the system resources. As a beginner, you will love GNOME, but it doesn't mean that advanced users dislike it. The environment can be configured according to your likings as it has quite a few advanced settings available. It's fairly unique, and it will not be fair to compare it with the latest desktop environments. If you are counting on appearance, it resembles more like Mac than Windows, and it is because the menu bar resides at the top whereas the task bar is at the bottom of the interface (especially in Ubuntu's new Unity interface).

KDE

K Desktop Environment (KDE) includes all the standard desktop features like file manager and window manager. It is a network-transparent desktop that has an exclusive set of applications that can do almost all Linux tasks. It is completely integrated with the internet as it is an internet aware system. Internet applications like Mailer, newsreader, and internet browser are available in KDE. The file manager also works as the Web and allows you to browse the internet directly. KDE serves a dual purpose; where it provides the ease of use for Windows and Macintosh, it brings the flexibility of the Linux operating system.

KDE is a bit heavier on the system resources, and also it is a bit more complex than GNOME. Instead of aiming to create an easy to use interface, KDE developers are always looking to evolve, and add more functionality to their prior KDE versions, affecting the beginners with these kinds of versions. However, its interface is very attractive, and it has an exciting desktop comprising of widgets. If you are counting on appearance, it resembles more like Windows, the task bar, and the main menu are located at the bottom of the interface. The main menu resides at the bottom left, and can be used if you want to launch applications or view settings. The complexity of KDE can be understood with the help of the following problems.

Firstly, it is very difficult to figure out where the settings you want to change are located. It is because there are various setting options and preference panes, which are pretty much confusing. Even if you are comfortable using Linux, or say computers, as a whole, you will still find it difficult to navigate. KDE offers various configuration options that are available in the main menu, but the problem arises that you cannot find the proper setting. Secondly, it also has some characteristics that can be confusing, especially for the beginners and new users. If you are dragging and dropping files anywhere, it always asks the user whether to move or copy that particular file, and it is that kind of problem which you can't seem to change. KDE is a great choice for the advanced users who are looking for a lot of configuration options, but there is always room for learning, and KDE will try to challenge their knowledge time to time.

Getting Started

Using Linux is quite easy as it provides a user friendly interface, which includes the graphical logins and GUIs (graphical user interfaces) like KDE and GNOME. It was difficult for the general public to interact with the command line interface but now even the standard Linux command line has become more user friendly. The commands can be edited, history list can be viewed, and the introduction of cursor-based tools has revolutionized the Linux system, as a whole.

There are two basic requirements of using Linux. The first requirement is that you should know how to access your Linux system, and secondly, you should know how to execute commands so that you can run the applications. Access can either be granted through the command line login or the default graphical desktop login. For the graphical login, a simple window pops up comprising of menus and options. The username and password can be fed in the appropriate fields to gain access. Once you gain access through the graphical login, you can interact with either the command line or a GUI. Interacting with GUI is quite easy as it comprises of the interface just like Windows.

The Shell

Shell is a type of an environment, but it can be considered as a separate entity. It interprets commands through a line-oriented interactive and non-interactive interface between the operating system and the user. The commands are entered on a command line, which is then interpreted by the shell and sent to the operating system as instructions. The commands can also be placed as script files which can be interpreted collectively. The shell is a program that controls the user's interaction. It is a process that allows the user to take complete control over the computer through the commands they type in the text interface. It is not a part of the kernel but uses it to create files, perform programs and much more. In simple words, it is the program that takes all the commands from the keyboard to the operating system.

Many different types of shells have been developed for Linux. Bourne Again shell (BASH), Korn shell, TCSH shell, and the Z shell are some of the prominent ones. A user only needs one type of shell to get the work done. BASH shell is set as default so you will be using this shell unless you specify or opt another.

Daemons

It is a program that runs as a background procedure. This program is not under the direct control of the user. Daemons controls the background services such as sound, printing, etc. that start during the boot or after you have logged into the desktop. The processes under this program end with the letter D. this clarifies that the procedure is a Daemon.

Applications

Where applications are concerned, the desktop environment does not offer the users with a number of options. Linux provides the users with millions of superior quality software titles, just like the MAC and Windows, that can be installed. The modern distributions that are included in Linux include tools that are similar to the App-store. These applications centralize and also make the installation procedure simple for you. For example, Ubuntu Software Center has millions of applications that you just have to install and not pay anything for.

Graphical Server

It is the system that holds half of the responsibility to display graphics on the screen. The Graphical Server is usually referred as X or the X server. It is made to act flexibly, and you can configure it in many ways. It works on all the window cards that are available. It is not limited to a specific desktop interface. It provides a range of graphical operations that file managers, window managers, and even desktops can use, among other user interface applications.

The Distribution

The Distribution is known to be the highest layer of the operating system. It is the program that contains all the layers as mentioned above. As the kernel is the first thing to get installed in the operating system, the distribution is the last. Without it, the system does not get completed. The makers of the Distribution layer decide which system tools, applications, kernel, and environment should be included to be used by the users.

There are several distributions of Linux although, there is one standard version of Linux. Different groups and companies have packaged Linux in a slightly different manner. The company releases the Linux package usually in the form of CD-ROM. They can later release the updated versions or new software. The kernel which is centrally used by all the distributions is acquired through kernel.org. Although the kernel used is the same, it can be configured differently by the distributers.

It is not very complicated to install the Distribution. It can be done with the help of a CD that contains the particular software for installation as well as configuration. The commercial companies or a professional individual either maintains this layer. For the convenience of the users, the best distributions offer them with a great application management system. This system will allow the users to find, and then install, the applications they want with just a few clicks of the mouse. This is the layer that makes searching simple, and an applications installation is just a few clicks away. Linux has 350 distributions available for the users. Listed below are the popular Linux distributions:

- Deepin

- Fedora

- Linux Mint

- Ubuntu Linux

- Debian

- Arch Linux

- OpenSUSE

Every distribution will have a dissimilar feeling and look on the monitor. A few have a contemporary user interface such as Deepin, Ubuntu, etc. On the other hand, others have a traditional environment such as OpenSUSE.

When you have Linux, you get all the choices. With the choices, also comes confusion. With many options available for Linux Desktop, which one is the most appropriate for you? Which desktop is the most user-friendly? There are no compulsory rules or tests that you need to follow to choose your desktop destination. It is all about your likes and features. When you look at the desktop functionality in detail, you will notice that there is certainly a connection between the desktop and the user. Mentioned below are the details of a few Linux desktops:

- *Ubuntu*

  Do you want a modern interface connecting to the local data as well as hundreds of remote sources? Users who wish to stay connected to social media want quick access to shopping websites, etc. will find Ubuntu as the best option. The users who would want to spend maximum time on the keyboard will prefer the Ubuntu Utility desktop. This form is certainly very efficient in interacting with the users. Ubuntu is the best choice for the users who want everything at their fingertips without caring a lot about the feel as well as the look of the desktop.

- *GNOME 3*

For the users who want a contemporary desktop with keeping the look and feel fresh, can choose GNOME 3. It has a minimalistic approach to an extensive desktop. On the desktop, you will not find many items which give you a feeling of minimal interaction. But when you open the dash, you will find plenty of interactive items. The Ubuntu locks some of the interfaces while this option allows tinkering. In case you are looking for a modern feel just like Ubuntu, but with some more tinkers, then GNOME 3 is made for you.

- ## *KDE Project*

  KDE Project is the distribution for KDE. A complete and developed desktop environment for the Linux operating system is KDE. This environment has had a few major changes that were required to be made for functionality. Thus, whatever the environment does, it does it brilliantly. It is the environment that has nothing else but the start menu, system tray, and panel. Since this environment has a modern touch, it still has some hold from the Windows generation, XP/7 to be precise. This option is perfect for those people who do not prefer change. Users who want the Windows design will prefer this environment because it is similar to Windows, but with a more modern look and simple transitions.

  ### *Enlightenment*

  It is an altogether different environment when compared to the others. While you initiate this environment, you start to notice the change. It is very different, as it does not have the start panel and menu, but a desktop menu and unique elements. However, this environment of the Linux OS is certainly not made for everyone. Those who want a unique, and ready to use simple environment can choose Enlightenment. Obviously, all of the uniqueness comes with a price tag. This desktop environment wants you to learn about it before you install so that it is not very tough for you to get a handle on it. Those who love to tinker with unique things will love this Linux desktop environment. Enlightenment comes with plenty of themes. The themes do not only have a changed desktop color but also a few changed details.

It is perfect for the user who loves change and wants a change on the desktop screen often.

- *Deepin*

The latest entry to the Linux operating system environments is Deepin. Just after the entry, this landscape has managed to attract a lot of people. It gives an amazingly modern look and feel to the desktop. The main thing about this landscape is that it combines all of the great desktops into one. It has a very attractive and unique control panel. The users will love exploring the new landscape. They will be pleased to find amazing features with a modern approach. Those looking out for a unique and simple landscape can have the best experience using this.

Chapter 2: Choosing a Linux Distribution System

Which distribution should you choose?

Finding the distribution that suits your needs will depend on the answers to the following questions:

- How experienced are you in using computers?

- What do you like – traditional or a modern desktop interface?

- Desktop or a server?

In case you possess average skills in using computers, then the latest and user-friendly distributions like Deepin, Ubuntu, and Linux Mint is the best choice. Fedora or Debian is the best option for all of those who possess above average computer skills. The distribution Gentoo is for all of the people who have mastered computers and are knowledgable about the system administration.

Are you looking out for a server-only distribution? If that is the case, then you will have to decide whether you want only the desktop interface or would like to do it with the help of the command line. GUI interfaces are not installed on the Ubuntu server. It means that you need to have a strong understanding of Linux operating system. Using a command of Sudo apt-get install ubuntu-desktop, you can install the GUI on the Ubuntu Server. Would you prefer a distribution that would offer you everything that you require for the server? CentOS is the perfect choice for such a case. Or, do you prefer a desktop distribution and then add on things as you like and need? Ubuntu Linux or Debain can be the right choice.

Following is the list of features the best Linux distributions have for new users:

User-friendly

This is one point where our debate can last forever. Thus, what should be done is, a new user should choose a distribution and start using it without a lot of explanation. In case there is a need to provide a detailed explanation, the distribution is certainly not user-friendly. For instance, any person without any coaching can start using the Windows 7 desktop. It is something every Linux desktop should consider.

App store

People are now getting too dependent on the mobile version, and they need to become accustomed to the app store on their home computer as well.

Applications

The basic necessities should be pre-installed, and users should not need to install them separately. So what are the necessities at present, as they keep changing often? Mentioned below are the applications that should come pre-installed:

- Email

- Music player

- Office Suite

- We browser

The list of applications to be installed depends on a person's needs.

Modern interface

There are many plenty attractive mobile landscapes, and thus, the desktop now needs to draw user's attention with a modern, unique and simple interface.

Ubuntu, Linux Mint, and Linux Deepin are the most commonly preferred distributions and following, is the ranking given to each of them according to the features:

User-friendliness

Rank 1 - Linux Mint

Rank 2 - Ubuntu Linux

Rank 3 - Linux Deepin

App store

Rank 1- Linux Deepin

Rank 2 - Linux Mint

Rank 3 - Ubuntu Linux

Applications

Rank 1- Linux Mint

Rank 2 - Ubuntu Linux

Rank 3 - Linux Deepin

Modern Interface

Rank 1- Linux Deepin

Rank 2 - Ubuntu Linux

Rank 3 - Linux Mint

According to your preferences and needs, you can choose the Linux distribution.

Where to obtain Linux Distribution

Along with providing a professional- level and stable Linux systems, the distributions provide the KDE and GNOME interfaces, hassle free and easy to use configuration tools, a variety of Internet services, an array of multimedia applications, and countless Linux applications of different types. Information about different distributions can be found at their respective websites. CDs and DVDs can be downloaded from these sites which can then be used to install Linux. Some distributions even provide live CDs which can be run on the

CD-ROM drive and you would not need to install it on your hard drive.

Distribution supported repositories also provide most of the software from the major distributions. They are available for downloading. Install disk images are available as both smaller desktop-only installs and large serve installs. Live-CD can be used to install Linux if provided.

The strategy for distribution includes the install disks and collection of software which can later be updated from the complete and diverse list of software on the distribution repositories. It means that you can start with the selection of software at a relatively smaller level. All the installations will have to undergo a constant update.

It is mandatory to read all the instructions for the distribution you're downloading. These can be found online on the website of the distribution and can be accessed through any browser.

What Defines a Linux Distribution?

Linux distribution is just not about the look and feel, but a lot of different things goes into making a distribution. While you're searching for the right distribution, you should take all those things into consideration. Most of these things can be installed separately, like if you don't like the apps or desktop environments of a particular distribution, you can install them individually. The idea of finding the right distribution means that you can find something that meets your ideal setup. You'll be spending less time and energy if you follow this approach. Here are some of the important points which you should keep in mind while choosing the distribution.

Package Managers

Package Manager or Package Management system helps you in maintaining the installation, upgradation, configuration and removal of computer programs consistently with the presence of a collection of software tools. It is one of the biggest features that differentiates various distributions. APT is the package manager for Ubuntu, and the same system is available on other distributions like Mint, Debian, etc. However, some distributions have their own package managers.

Yum manager (Fedora) for instance is easier to use through command line as compared to APT. It can be slower at times, though.

Where ease of use matters, the availability of a particular package manager should also be kept in mind. Fedora is not as popular as other distribution using APT so it can be difficult for you to find the exact app you're looking for. You'll have to build it from sources instead of getting it directly through repositories. While it is easier to build from sources, you'll get stuck when you are not able to update when a new version is released automatically. So, you have to take into account both the ease of use and accessibility of the package manager.

Desktop Environment

We have already seen different desktop environments, their differences and how they are important to the overall working of the Linux system. While choosing the right distribution, the desktop environment should be kept in mind. Some of the important things about desktop environments can be recalled here to understand how it affects your choice for the right distribution.

These includes things like:

- The overall look and feel of your windows, menus and desktop and its overall customizability.
- The usage of resource
- Different options available in your distribution's graphical preferences (like changing the items you want to appear in your menus or remapping of certain keys).
- The overall integration of different programs with your desktop.

Although a separate desktop environment can be installed, no one can deny its importance while choosing the distribution. You will save time if the default desktop environment is close to what you want, you'll not have to install it separately. It will also work in a better with the rest of the programs.

Stability vs. Cutting Edge

Distributions have a specific release and update cycles. While some keep updating and provide the most up to date version of apps and packages, others delay the upgrade process to ensure stability. Fedora, provides the latest and greatest by giving the most up to date versions, whereas Debian, will intentionally delay the release of certain updates to make everything is running smoothly. So you have the option of choosing according to your preference. You can go for Fedora if you enjoy the latest versions of Firefox or any other app. If stability is your priority, then sticking to Debian would be the best option.

Hardware Compatibility

Different distributions package drivers differently, this is to say that the printer compatibility will depend on the distribution you choose. Some printers might work for one distribution, but not for another. Although, you can install drivers separately for your printer, you can save time and effort by finding a distribution that supports your printer. Other things like Wi-Fi, sound, and video cards should be checked for compatibility from the hardware compatibility pages of the distribution. If you find it there, then you are good to go or else you will have to put a little extra to install drivers.

Community Support

Community Support has become an important aspect in my fields today. Finding the right answers easily through these forums can solve your problem, and you no longer have to be annoyed at issues which you can't resolve by yourself. Linux is no different, and community support is a big help for Linux users. While choosing the right distribution, you should check the community surrounding it. Troubleshooting help, app support, or even generic information is essential for beginners. It is this one aspect that has made Ubuntu a popular choice as a distribution. You can search for different forums for distributions and choose the one you find most helpful and providing the best support.

The Must-Use Distributions

After discovering the factors which constitute in your choice for the distribution, the next step is exploring the options. 'DistroWatch' is an excellent resource to find different distributions. The number of distributions is in hundreds so you can find the information overwhelming. Below is the list compiled of some of the most popular distributions, but you can feel free to explore other options. Although these distributions offer a variation of the desktop environment, we will stick to the default one to make it simple.

Ubuntu (Standard)

Ubuntu is a great distribution for beginners. It is made with an aim to make Linux easier to use for average person – which it has fulfilled. It is updated every six months and extremely easy to use. It has its own Unity interface which offers unique features like dock instead of a taskbar, and the package manager is in the form of an App Store like the interface and a dashboard which makes searching process easier. Although most of the people like it, you always have the option to bring it back to the GNOME interface if you like. The standard apps which come with Ubuntu include Firefox, Empathy (instant messaging), Thunderbird, and other apps like Transmission for downloading torrents. You won't have to build from source as Ububtu has a great hardware compatibility. The community support for Ububtu is the best, so if you're looking for a hassle-free option, Ububtu should be your pick.

Linux Mint (Made for beginners)

Although Linux Mint is based on Ububtu, it has gained popularity separately, especially after the introduction of the Unity interface by Ububtu. The purpose of Mint Linux is to make the process as simple as possible for people who are not familiar with Linux. The menus are easy to use, and the installation process is hassle-free. Many applications like Adobe Flash, MP3 support, and other hardware drivers come preinstalled, and you don't have to install them separately like you have to do for other distributions. The default or preinstalled apps are similar to that of Ubuntu (with Pidgin taking the place of Empathy for instant messaging). The package manager followed is the same as Ububtu, which gives you the ease of access to different programs available in repositories. The community support is extensive as novice mostly use this distribution. Linux Mint is highly recommended if you've never used Linux before.

Fedora (Bleeding Edge User)

Fedora is known for its up to date and cutting edge software. The updates usually come out after six months, as is the case with Ubuntu, but unlike Ubuntu, those updates are not supported for a longer period. The users are expected to update as soon as possible. If Mozilla releases an update for Firefox, the programs will be updated immediately in Fedora, while Ubuntu makes specific changes to the program before releasing the update. This consistent update can result in some instability, but people who always prefer the latest version don't care much about this. It is the most popular Linux distribution which can be easily updated to GNOME. Ubuntu and Mint's ATP is somewhat harder to use as compared to the slow, but easier to use Yum package manager. The software availability is not as extensive as that found in Ubuntu or Mint, and you can still get most of the software through repositories. The enterprise and security features of Fedora makes it popular for use in the professional environment. Serious Linux users will definitely prefer Fedora.

Debian (Cautious and Stable)

Debian is opposite to Fedora in many ways. Its aim is to remain as stable as possible – which it does adeptly. The downside is that your system is not up to date, most of the times. The new releases come out after 1 to 3 years, but if you don't care much about having the latest version, and are content with stability, Debian is the right pick for you. The package management system used by Debian is the same as that of Ubuntu and Mint, which means that you will get most of the programs, and you don't have to checkout repositories. If you have an old or offbeat build, you're going to like Debian as it supports many processor architectures.

OpenSUSE (Made for Tinkerer)

OpenSUSE has a really helpful community and a general purpose Linux distribution. The level of configuration it offers makes it stand out from other distributions. While KDE is the default desktop, you get the option of choosing from different desktops like KDE, GNOME, XFCE and LXDE while you're installing. The added benefits of OpenSUSE is a good system administration utility and package manager (YaST) and the ease of access to documentation through the community. Opting KDE and OpenSUSE means that it can be resource heavy, so you need to make sure that you have sufficient resources before making the decision. If you want to have the freedom of choice, you can get it by choosing OpenSUSE as it offers many configuration options, and you wouldn't have to delve into the command line.

Arch Linux (For the Adamant)

Arch Linux requires you to start from scratch. It doesn't have many characteristics of its own, and you make everything, by yourself. All you have when you start is the command line. From this, you build your desktop environment, applications you prefer, drivers and all other things you need along the way. You're making a customized distribution of Arch Linux. It takes a lot of work and effort but the result is what's important for you. You will learn a great deal through the process. It is a great learning experience as you will be able to figure out in case something went wrong (with the help of the community, it is usually really helpful).

The 'Pacman' package manager is used by Arch which is extremely powerful. You are always up to date with the last versions. Arch User Repository (AUR) is a great platform where installable versions of all the programs are built by the community. Although it is not an official platform, you can get to install all the programs you might need with AUR helper, just like normal packages in the repositories.

There are many other Linux distributions as well like Slackware or CentOS. There are also variations of these basic distributions like LXDE-enabled Lubuntu (which is based on Ubuntu as the name suggests). You can start with the basic ones but is recommended that you try different distributions as it will only help you learn a lot about Linux, but you would understand your needs in a better way.

Chapter 3: Installing Linux

People think that installing the Linux operating system is a very tough task to do. In fact, it is known to have the simplest installations when compared to the other operating systems. Most of the Linux operating system versions offer you with the Live Distribution. It means that the installation can be done with the help of a CD or USB without making any huge changes in your hardware. Isn't this just amazing? These distribution options provide you with the full functionality without having to install it forever.

For example, following are the steps for Ubuntu Linux that will guide you through the installation process:

- Preparation

  The first thing to ensure is that your machine meets the requirements. It might ask you whether you want to install third party software.

- Wireless setup

  When you install the system on the laptop, you will have to connect to a network to ensure that download of third party software is successful.

- Hard drive allocation

  It is the step where you need to choose the way you want the Linux operating system to be installed on your desktop or laptop. Are you going to go with dual booting? Then use the whole hard drive, upgrade the present installation.

Choose the kind of installation you would prefer and then click on install now.

- Location: choose location from map

- Keyboard setup: choose the keyboard setup

- User setup: type in your username and password to finish installation

After these steps are followed, reboot and then it is ready to go! Installing Linux is known to be the simplest, as well as the safest, the software when compared to other operating systems.

Important considerations while installing Linux

Installing Linus is pretty easy as almost every distribution has its own graphical install scheme. Nowadays, installation is a piece of cake, and it involves only a few clicks. As the software data has grown enormous over the years, so that is why most of the distributions only provide the basic material for running the Linux in the shape of CD and DVD. Distributions further provide links to the online repositories which can be downloaded later, after the primary installation from CD and DVD. Installation now is a mere setting of initial configuration which can be enhanced later by downloading the specific drivers of your choice from the online repositories. Many distributions also provide you with the freedom of creating your own install discs. You can install the software of your likings in your own CD/DVD.

Some important installation considerations include the following.

- Software available on CD's and DVD's is prone to outdating. Thus, the need for online repositories becomes critical as it is helpful for downloading and updating the software.
- Some distributions keep on updating their original releases now and then. These updated versions are available on their respective sites, and must be checked for their availability.
- Hardware is mostly automatically detected nowadays. It includes your monitor and graphic cards etc.
- Most distributions provide Parted (partition management tool). It's very easy to use and helps you in setting up your partitions.
- A number of sources can be utilized for the installation purpose. For instance, network methods like NFS, Hypertext Transfer Protocol (HTTP, and File Transfer Protocol (FTP).
- Boot managers like GRUB or Linux Loader (LILO) usually support the dual-boot installation. These boot loaders can be

easily configured to boot Mac, Windows, and other Linux installations on the same system.

- Distributions deal 32-bit and 64-bit as separate entities and provide their different releases. Newer computers support 64-bit nowadays, whereas weaker systems support 32-bit.
- Dynamic Configuration Protocol (DHCP) or IPv6 helps in connecting to a network router, and this network configuration is normally automatic.
- RAID and LVM file systems can be set up during installation, as you have the option to customize your partitions using Parted.
- It's extremely vital to have a separate boot partition if you are using LVM and Raid file systems.
- Most distributions also run a post-installation process. It helps in performing the basic configuration tasks like creating a user account, setting the date and time, and also configuring your firewall.

Linux system can be accessed in rescue mode, and most distributions provide this facility. If your system stops working, your install disc can be used to access your files. Your install disc uses the command line interface and helps you access your installed file system. The configuration files can be edited and replaced, and it allows you to fix your problem. This technique is useful for X Window System.

GRUB boot loader is prone to glitches, especially if you install Windows on your system. It happens because Windows overwrite your boot manager. GRUB can be reinstalled utilizing the grub install command, and once you have installed it, be sure to mark that for Windows system. It should be noted that alternative boot loaders like LILO are used by some distribution.

What are the reasons to use the Linux operating system?

Why would you want to learn a computing program that is completely different when the laptop, desktop, and other servers are shipped with the Operating System that works perfectly? This is the question that comes up in most of the users' minds. Before you get an answer to this, there is one more question, is the operating system you are working on really working as perfectly as you wanted? Are you frequently battling with slowdowns, viruses, expensive repairs and malware? If yes, then it is the right time to free yourself from the constant frustration, as well as fear of losing your important data. Linux is the best solution for you and you need to start using this operating system at your earliest convenience.

Linux is known to be an operating system that is most reliable. You get a reliable operating system by paying nothing, seriously. You can install Linux on as many laptops or desktops you want for free.

When Linux is compared to the other servers such as Windows Server, the latter costs around $1200 and does not include the basics like Client Access License and also other licenses including mail server, web server, etc. the Linux Server is free and you do not have to pay a cent to use its reliable programs. It is free and also simple to install. When you have Linux as the operating system, you do not have to do babysitting every day. There is one service that needs restarting, upgrading, etc. and the other parts are not affected.

This operating system is distributed under the open source license and mentioned below is a list of ideas that it follows:

The liberty to run any program.

The liberty to make changes to the programs according to your preference.

You can even redistribute copies to help your loved ones.

Lastly, you can distribute the copies of the modified version that you created to your loved ones.

Thus, it is a community that is created by you, for you. It is known to be the simplest and most user-friendly operating system. It is all about freedom. Complete Linux installation can be done on your desktop or laptop as it does not involve a lot of complexities.

Development

The Linux operating system includes a number of development languages. Most of the distribution codes are created in C or C++

Languages. The rest of the codes are created with Perl, Java as well as Lisp. One of the most important parts of the Linux operating system, The Kernel has 95% C presence. The remaining part is used with other languages that make this part more diverse when compared to the other systems.

There are a few developers that at present use text-based tools to develop the code. Linux is known to be the most versatile operating system and a strong integrated development environment. It is a platform that can help you generate money while being free of cost. Users can be certain that the Linux operating system can work best for them.

Chapter 4: File Systems for Linux

As almost everyone is familiar with the fact that the files reside on physical storage devices such as hard drives, floppy disks, or CD-ROMs. In Linux, file system comprises of the collection of files on each storage device in an organized form. The collection of the file system on storage devices is presented as data and thus, can be managed by you. If you are willing to add a new storage device, it is needed to be attached to your Linux file structure as a separate file system. Hard drives can be allocated to separate storage device called partitions. Each partition has its own file system. A number of administrative tasks can be performed on your file systems. You can simply back your file system, attach or detach them from your file structure, and new devices can be formatted, and the older ones can be removed, and the file system can be checked for problems and glitches.

Attaching the file system to a specified directory in order to access files on a device is referred as mounting the file system. For instance, if you want to access files on a hard drive, you have first to mount its file system on a specific directory. A number of different types of file systems can be mounted in Linux. You always have the right to access the Windows hard drive partition, tape drive, and file systems on a remote server can also be accessed.

File systems are one of the layers underneath your operating system. It is something that is usually not considered unless one is faced with the plethora of alternatives in Linux. It is essential to know how to make a well-informed decision on which file system needs to be used.

The landscape of the file systems support of Linux is completely different from that of OS X and Windows. As far as Windows and OS X are concerned, there is software that will add support for non-standard file systems. However, both operating systems can be installed on their native file system, and third party support is then added.

On the other hand, Linux has an enormous range of supported file systems developed into the kernel. But the main question is how to know which file system to select at the time of installation. There are some of the very popular choices available. However, the choice completely depends on the requirements.

What Is Journaling?

Before going ahead with file system options, it is essential first to have a quick check on journaling. One of the significant things about journaling is that all of the modern file systems makes use of journaling in one or another form, and on any desktop or laptop that you are setting up with Linux. This is where it is essential to use the journaling file system.

Only when writing to disk, journaling is utilized. With this, the issue of disk corruption can be fixed at the time things are written to the hard drive and after that if the computer crashes or when there is a loss of power. The operating system, without the journal, will not be able to in know if the file was completely written to the disk.

With the use of journaling, the file will first be written to the journal, enter it and then the journal will write a file to the disk when it is ready. After it has been successfully written to the disk, it will be removed from the journal, then punch out and the operation will be finished.

In case there is a loss of power at the time of being written to the disk, the file system can check out the journal for all operations which have not been finished and remember where it left off.

The major downside to journaling is that it will compromise some performance in substitute for stability. In order to write a file, there is lots of overhead. However, the file system will go around this overhead. It is possible through not writing the complete file to a journal. Rather than this, the file metadata, inode or disk location is recorded prior to being written to disk.

Journaling allows you to recover your files from a crash or interruption quite easily. The Reiser FS, ext3, XFS, and JFS file systems are built-in with the ability to maintain a record of files and directory changes. It is referred to as a journal. The journal helps in recovering the files when the system suddenly crashes in response to some unforeseen events such as power failure.

The Reiser FS and ext3 were the file systems that introduced journaling ability to Linux systems. The e2fsck and fsck file systems are slower in response, but journaling provides fast, efficient and precise recovery of files in case of disk crashes. A journal file maintains the log of all file system actions. In the case of a crash, Linux only needs to find and read the journal file, and then replay it so that the system can regenerate the file to its original stable state. Those files that were still in the process of writing on the disk can also be restored to their original state. As mentioned above, that the fsck file system is slower as it checks each file and directory manually, and also it takes several minutes to check on reboots when your system accidently shuts down. Journaling, on the other hand, skips the lengthy process, and it just reads the journal files to restore the file system to its original state.

Journaling is far much better, and even faster method to restore files than the other non-journal methods. Almost all journaling systems record and maintain a file system directory structure, and it is known as the metadata. Metadata offers different levels of file data recovery. File system's response time can be slowed down as the maintenance of file data recovery information is a time consuming task. Journaling systems prove to be more quick and efficient in recovering the file systems, providing a prompt response time than the traditional non-journal file system.

Accessing Your Linux System

It is important to note that proper startup and shutdown procedures should be followed in order to use Linux system. You cannot just switch off your computer. Journaling is implemented by Linux which can allow recovering after the system has been shut down automatically, in the case of loss of power.

When you turn on or reset your system, the boot loader GRUB decides which operating system to load and run. The GRUB will then display a list of operating systems from which you can choose. If you press any key in the meantime or wait for longer than usual, the default operating system is loaded.

The Linux operating system can be thought of working at two levels. At the initial level, you can't interact with it. It is the level where you start your Linux system and wait for the system to load and run. After the system has started, it displays a login screen, waiting for you to login and start using the system. The system can't be accessed without the login. After you have logged in, you enter the next level. You can now give commands to the system to perform different tasks, be it the use of editors or compilers, use of different programs or even games. You can interact with the system either by command line interface or directly from the desktop. There are two types of login; command line login prompts and graphical login windows. Most of the distributors have graphical interface login asking for your username and password as default. If you opt out of using the graphical interface, you are given the simple command line prompt where you just have to enter your username.

File System Options

There are a few of the major file systems available for Linux. It is essential for you to know briefly about these systems as it gives an idea of when you might and might not want to use the specific file system on the basis of the features. This does not imply that the file systems cannot be utilized in other cases. These are actually some suggestions where every file system will stand out.

Ext4

In case you have installed Linux prior, there are chances that you might have seen the Ext4 during installation. There is one good reason behind this, and that is because it is the file system of choice for almost all Linux distribution available. The fact is that there are few who choose other options for file systems. However, the Ext4 is the file system of choice for almost every user of Linux.

What can this file system do?

Extended 4 has all that is expected in comparison to the past file systems interactions such as Ext2 or Ext3. This file system has a lot of enhancements. There are a lot of things that this file system can do. However, here are some of the best things that this file system can do for you:

- Journal checksums

- File system journaling

- Backward compatibility support for Ext2 and Ext3

- Enhanced file system checking in comparison to previous versions

- Offers support for large files

- Multi-block file allocation

- Constant pre-allocation of free space

Who can make use of this file system?

The Ext4 file system is best for the people that are in search of a super-stable base to develop upon, or for those searching for something that just works. It is the system that would not take a snapshot of your system, and it also does not have the best SSD support. However, in case your requirements are not too much, then you will just be to do well with it.

XFS

XFS is one of the high-end file systems created by Silicon Graphics. It is the system that specializes in performance and speed. When parallel input and output is concerned, this file system can run amazingly well. The reason behind this is that it concentrates on performance. It is the file system that can tackle an excessive amount of data. The fact is, this file system can handle around 300+ terabytes of data.

What can this file system do?

This file system is one of the well-tested data storage systems developed for great performance operation. This system can do following things:

- File system journaling

- Direct I/O

- Guaranteed rate I/O

- Online defragmentation

- Changeable block sizes

- Snapshots

- Lined allocation of RAID arrays

- Online resizing

Who can make use of this file system?

Those that are searching for a rock solid file system, this is the best one. This system has been around since 1993 and over time, it has become much better. In case you have a home server, and you are concerned about the storage, then considering XFS can be a good option. This is not only for servers. In the case that you are a more advanced user, then this can also be a good option. This does not have a stability problem.

BtrFS

This file system for Linux is created through Oracle. This is one of the newer file systems. The Linux Company considers it as unbalanced, as it is in the development stage. This file system is dependent on the principle of 'copy on write' concept. This concept implies that the system has one single copy of data before the data has been written. At the time data has been written, there will be a copy made.

What can this file system do?

There are a lot of things can be done through BtrFS system. Here are some of the things this system can do:

- Supports read-only snapshots

- Subvolumes

- File cloning

- Offline file system check

- Transparent compression

- Online defragmentation

- Support for RAID 0, RAID1, RAID 1, RAID 5, RAID 6 and RAID 10

Who can make use of this file system?

The makers of BtrFS say that this file system is the next-generation replacement for other file systems available, but it is still a work in progress. There are a lot of great features for basic and advanced users. It is great for the people who want more from the file system and want to have their hands on a 'copy on write' way.

Reiser4

This is the file system that is a successor to ReiserF5, and it is developed by Namesys. The development of Reiser4 was supported through the Linspire project and DARPA. Another thing that makes this file system great is its multitude of transaction models. There is not only one way through which data can be written, and rather there are many.

What can this file system do?

It is the system that has an innovative ability to utilize various transaction models. This is the system that makes use of 'copy-on write' models, write anywhere, hybrid transaction model and journaling. Following are some of the things that this system can do:

- Better support for smaller files

- Faster handling of directories

- Better system journaling through wandering logs

- Huge improvement over ReiserF5

Apart from this, there are other features also, but in short, it can be said that it is a huge enhancement over ReiserFS with a lot of other features.

Who can use this file system?

If a person is searching to stretch one file system throughout the multiple use-cases, then Reiser4 is the best option. This can be a good option if you want to have one machine with copy-on-write, another with write-anywhere and another with the hybrid transaction. It is a good choice if you do not want to utilize various kinds of file systems for completing the task. This is one of the best for this kind of cases.

There are many file systems available for Linux. All of these serve a distinctive purpose for different users searching to solve various issues.

Chapter 5: Linux Text Editors

Linux distributions are comprised of a number of applications, referred to as text editors. They can be used to develop text files or edit system configuration files. These editors are similar to word processing programs. However, normally it has fewer features, works only with text files and may or may not support checking of spelling and formatting.

These text editors have some features and are simple to use. They are normally found on all Linux distributions. The number of editors installed over your system is based on which software packages you have installed on the system.

Reasons Why You Should Use Text Editors

Linux is a highly file-centric operating system which means that everything is a file. All fundamental configurations are done through carefully designed text files in the correct place with the correct content. You can find many graphical tools for configuring Linux box. However, the majority of these just twist files for you.

The text files have a specific syntax that you need to follow. A simple character that is omitted can expose your system to risk. Using a word processor for this is not a good idea. This can actually corrupt your files with additional formatting information. File configuration does not require italic or bold fonts it just requires correct information.

The same thing applies to the source code. Compilers are strict regarding syntax. Few of them also consider where the particular command is. Word processors will mess up the text position in the lines of code. It is essential for you to have a clear understanding what is in the source code or configuration file, to know whether the system will understand exactly what you are writing.

If you are considering coding, then you will want to use an Integrated Development Environment. With this, it can help you write code more efficiently because it can predict what you would like to type, suggest changes or also show your mistakes. This can color specific keywords and automatically place things in the correct place.

The coloring and highlighting are done within the display. These kinds of changes are done to the text files that are meant to be the plain text. It is one of the best features that you cannot get with word processing programs, and this is required for text editing.

Conventionally, most Linux distributions just stick to install the editors like Vim and Emacs, as they are cursor based and easy to use. Vim is the advanced version of Vi text editor that was employed on the Unix system. These editors are user friendly, and they let the user work with ease on the cursor-based operations allowing to give a full screen format. These kinds of editors do not require any X Window system support and be initiated from the shell command line. However, in this mode, the working is not that easy because of the fact that there are no menus, mouse-click options, and scroll bar. Although, KDE and GNOME support the text editors with all the vital features. Using the text editors with the desktop environments is just like working on Windows and Macintosh systems. They provide the user with full mouse support, elaborative and exciting menus, and scroll bars. You may find these editors much easier to use as compared to Vi and Emacs. The editors can run on either desktop environments, whether it is KDE or GNOME. You must have pre-installed environments to use the editors.

Linux Text Editors

Linux has many of text editors available when it comes to simple text, structured text and programming languages. Here are some of the most popular listed, and all of these are available for a wide range of operating systems.

Linux Text Editors For Plain Text

Linux text editors for plain text are segregated into two categories that are graphical editors. The two categories are GUI and console text editors. The benefit of the GUI editor is that it is an intuitive, user-friendly interface. On the other hand, the advantage of console text editor is the suitability for long distance network connection which may or may not offers appropriate bandwidth or reliability.

Console Based Text Editors

Emacs

This text editor supports the concept that more is better. It is something that tries to support all features as far as possible. In case you want power then try Emacs. Through this, you can actually get unrestricted open files and sub-windows, shell access and immoral way with scripts you can call out the keywords, are defining features of Emacs.

There are many variations of Emacs available that is suitable for major programming languages used for text highlighting of programming keywords as it is done for coding. When you have an Emacs session open you can write, code, email or also play arcade games.

Along with that, Emacs has its own onboard assistance system with excessive capabilities that are comprised of the user-defined development of new commands that you will never require leaving. Some of the good things about this are that it is powerful, customizable and extensible. This allows you to express your own creativity.

Jed

Jed is one of the text editors that support menus and other GUI features in the console based terminal. This text editor mainly focuses on software development. One of the best features is that it is rich in Unicode mode. It is also extremely lightweight which means that it will not exert pressure on the system resource, making it ideal for older systems.

Pico

The Pico text editor was developed to assist users in speeding their email along with the pine email system. This text editor has lots of commands available which is displayed at the bottom of the text editing area to help. It is very easy to use, and it offers many basic features like paragraph justification, spelling checker and copy/paste.

The interface is pretty much similar to that of Notepad in the Windows.

Nano

The Nano text editor is done over small and amazing design goals for making an open source version of Pico. There are some additional features such as search, replace and smooth scrolling. This editor also lets you use a mouse and other printer devices for positioning of the cursor or activate commands over the shortcuts bar at the bottom of the screen. It is keyboard oriented, and you can perform many functions using the Control (Ctrl) keys.

Vim

Vim is one of the console-based plain text editors that supports syntax highlighting and has many plug-ins for specialized features and configurations. It is one of the standard Linux editors. This has been a part of Linux from the beginning. It is possible to duct in and duct out in just a few seconds which rapidly changes the text files. More recent Vim extensions provide additional functionality comprising of new editing commands and mouse support and graphical versions. You can find a tutorial for beginners which is built in and can be accessed through 'vimtutor' command. Vim user manual is also available which enlists the features. It can be accessed either within Vim or online.

Graphical GUI Editors

Gedit

It is one of the default text editors for Linux Gnome desktop. It is the editor that has search and replace functionality, undo and redo and work with several structural languages. This is the one that supports syntax highlighting, a variety of plug-ins, printing, multi-language spell check, tabbed for multiple files, etc. An extra feature of this editor is that it comprises of automatically detecting and alerting you of changes to an open file through another application. It is a highly popular and efficient text editor, and the limitations can be avoided through available plugins.

NEdit

It is one of the original Unix GUI text editors that are programmed in Motif. This is mainly a fundamental intuitive and simple to use GUI editor. It only not helps in intensive and continuous editing but is also easy to learn and a handy option for casual use. The interface is similar to the text editors offered by Windows and Macintosh.

Gvim

This is the one that offers a GUI editor on the basis of the vim console editor. There are lots of features offered through this GUI text editor. However, it will still need knowledge regarding vim so that you do not run into trouble.

Sublime

Sublime is a commercial GUI text editor which features syntax highlighting, plain text, cross-platform, C++ and Python language support and plain text. It offers many other features like column selection and multi-select editing, auto completion (depending on the language and variables created by the user), snippets, auto save and much more.

Tea

The Text Editor of the Atomic Era (TEA is an acronym) is the Qt based GUI text editor that supports cross platform, syntax highlighting, plain text, regular expression search and replace, file manager, programming language, etc.

Structured Text Editors

Structured text mainly refers to logical formatting and annotated text for representing program function or data schema. In this, there are two common formats available, and they are HTML for text documents and XML for data representation.

HTML Text Editors

Amaya

This is one of the fundamental and simple to use editors. In order to be complete, it will require more features. It offers many features like Access keys, page zooming, password management, spell checking and much more.

Kompozer

This editor is a simple to use GUI HTML editor. There are a lot of features that this editor can offer, and it was renamed from Nvu.

Quanta

It is one of the editors that also offers support to programming languages such as Python, SQL, Perl, PHP, etc. It offers features like project management, plugins, integrated preview and context help. It is highly configurable, and you can set it according to your needs with diverse settings offered by Quanta.

Bluefish

Bluefish text editor is one that also supports XML markup and also programming languages. It can either work as a standalone application or can be put to use via integration with GNOME. It is easy to learn and lightweight. It has been translated into 17 languages. Some prominent features include syntax highlighting, multiple document support, auto completion, code folding, advance search and replace, etc.

Aptana

Aptana is a GUI HTML editor that offers support to VSS, Ruby, PHP and Javascript that comprises of debugging. It is a cross platform and Java based editor.

Coffee Cup

This is a commercial HTML editor, and it is developed in validation. It is the one that supports HTML5 and CSS3.

XML Editors

Oxygen XML

It is a commercial cross-platform GUI XML or Eclipse plug-in editor. For files of this kind, this has proved to be a capable editor with a clear validation warning and error messages.

Eclipse

This is the cross-platform Java IDE that supports DTD or XSD or XSLT or XML. It is one of the efficient editors. However, it is not good at verification of XSD and XML.

Emacs nXML mode

This editor allows a schema that is related to XML document that is being edited. It offers continuous support validation.

Kate

Knowing Kate is very easy. The learning curve is gentle in comparison to other well-known Linux text editors and comprises of the best features. This comprises of a span of text editor needs for basic text writing and integrated development environment. It is a KDE application that is good for KDE users and also for GNOME users.

Along with that, the Linux users that make use of Windows or Mac OSX will be glad to know that this text editor will be able to run under these operating systems in the best possible manner. With this text editor, Window or pane splitting is available, and there is a possibility of personalizing the functionality of this text editor for various kinds if projects. The only problem with this plug-in is that it is not simple to find, this runs great under KDE.

Chapter 6: Linux Commands

Linux commands are one of the biggest strengths of Linux based systems. The main reason behind this is that it makes it simple for the user to interact with their system. Linux commands also save resources of the system that is consumed by GUIs. For the slower systems, it is always better to be good with the command lines than GUI. Linux command lines offer flexibility, speed, and a great experience.

Command Line Interface (CLI)

Command line interface act as a bridge between the user and computer program. The user simply inputs the instructions in the command prompt (a dialogue box) in the form of successive lines of text, and in return, the program is executed. Even with GUI, you sometimes need to have command line interface in order to execute the commands. GNOME desktop menu is not provided with The Terminal Window option now, and they can be accessed from the Applications | System Tools menu. But you need not be worried about it if you use Terminal windows option frequently. The option can be dragged to the desktop from the menu, and can be used whenever required by just clicking it.

Linux commands are based on options and arguments, and if you fail to keep the correct order, your command may not execute. So, it is extremely important to place the options and arguments in the right order. Linux commands follow the simple rule, and the correct format of a command is as follows.

$ *command-name options arguments*

An option is a one-letter code, and it is usually preceded by one or two hyphens, which transforms the type of action the command performs. Depending upon the type of command, options and arguments may or may not be optional. Let's have a look at an example; the **Is** command can be written as **−s** considering an option. This could be broken down into two steps. Firstly, the **Is** command lets you have a look at the listing of files in your directory, and secondly, the **–s** option lets you see the size and space of each file in blocks. The correct format for this command must be as follows.

$ ls –s

An argument, on the other hand, is the data that is necessary for the command to execute its task. In most cases, it is a file name. The argument comes after the option and is entered in the form of words. For instance, if you want to display the contents of a file, you can use the **less** and **more** command with the file's name. The correct format to display the contents of a file named **mydata** can be fed as

$ less mydata

The command line can be edited easily, and it is very simple to add or remove the commands. Just before pressing the ENTER button, you can perform changes in the pre- existing commands. It provides flexibility and ease as you can correct the mistakes you make while typing the command and its options and arguments. You can simply erase the characters with the help of BACKSPACE and DEL keys. Utilizing this ability, you can erase the whole command in a line. An alternative method can be opted to erase a line which is a shortcut key (CTRL-U). It erases the line letting you start over again.

Accessing Linux from the Command Line Interface

While working with command line interface, you are initially provided with a login prompt. It indicates that the system is running, and is in search of a user to login. You can simply add your username and password in the respective fields to proceed. Once you have provided this information you are now eligible to use the system. Before showing up the login prompt, the command line shows the hostname you gave to your system. For instance, consider the hostname as **bird** in this case. When you have performed your task, you can log out. Linux then displays the exact login prompt, and will wait for another user to login again.

Linux release

Kernel 2.6 on an i686

bird login:

Once you entered your account, you can now enter and execute commands. The two primary requirements of log in must be fulfilled. For instance, as in our case, we take the username as micolp. After entering the username, the user is prompted to enter the password.

Linux release

Kernel 2.6 on an i686

bird login: micolp

While you are entering the password, it does not appear on the screen. It is to protect your password from others. If either the password or username is entered incorrectly, the system will reply with the error "Login incorrect." It will start the log in the process all over again, and once you have provided the correct username and password, you can now work with the system. Another important thing to mention here is that the command line prompt is a dollar sign ($), and it is not a number sign (#). Regular users use the $ sign prompt, whereas the # sign is only limited to the root users. In this version of Linux, the hostname and directory you are in, are bounded by a set of brackets.

[bird / home/ micolp]$

To terminate your session, you have to provide the exit command. This redirects you to the log in prompt, and Linux will now wait for the next user to log in.

[bird / home/ micolp]$ **logout**

Shutting Down Linux Using the Command Line

Turning off your computer requires you first to shut down your Linux. If you are not shutting down your Linux properly, it may perform lengthy system checks when you want to start up again. The system can be shut in either of the two ways. The first method is quite simple, just log in to an account and provide the system with the halt command. This command will terminate all the on-going processes, and will log you out shutting down the system.

$ halt

In contrary, you can give the shutdown command with the **−h** option. You can also provide an alternative option that is **−r** which shuts down the system and then reboots it.

If you want to shut down the system immediately, you can use the option **+o** or by entering the word **now**.

 # shutdown -h now

You should be aware that turning off the computer directly could be detrimental, as shutting down leads to the unmounting file systems, and is also responsible for the closing down of any servers.

Another shutting technique can also be utilized. It is more of a forced shut down. It is achieved by holding the CTRL and ALT keys simultaneously, and then pressing the DEL key. Your system will then follow the standard shutdown procedure, and then will reboot itself.

Starting a GUI Utilizing the Command Line

It does not matter if you have logged in from the command line, you still have the option to shift to X Window system GUI such as GNOME, KDE (desktop environments). The desktop can be seen by giving the command **startx**. GNOME is usually selected by default. GNOME desktop is initiated on giving the command. The right format to execute the desktop is:

$ startx

Given below is the list of the basic commands which you should know as a starter.

ls [option(s)] [file(s)]

>   The contents of the current directory will be displayed in short form by the program if you run **ls** without the use of any additional parameters.

>   -l

>   Depicts the detailed list

-a

Displays any hidden files

cp [option(s)] sourcefile targetfile

Copies sourcefile to targetfile.

-i

Delays for validation, if necessary, before an
existing targetfile is overwritten

-r

Duplicates recursively (includes sub-directories)

mv [option(s)] sourcefile targetfile

Duplicates sourcefile to targetfile and then deletes the
original sourcefile.

-b

Before moving, it creates a backup copy of the sourcefile

-i

Delays for validation, if necessary, before an
existing targetfile is overwritten

rm [option(s)] file(s)

It helps in removing the specified files from the file system.
However, directories are not removed by **rm,** but can be
removed by the use of option -r.

-r

Erases any existing sub-directories

-i

Delays for validation before deleting each file.

ln [option(s)] sourcefile targetfile

The command can be utilized to create an internal link under a different name. These links are created from the sourcefile to the targetfile, and normally these links indicate directly to the one and the same file system. However, if **ln** command is executed using

−s option, it forms a link that indicates the point where the source file is located in a directory. It is how the linking across the file system is enabled.

-s

Creates a symbolic link

cd [options(s)] [directory]

It changes the current directory. **cd** without any parameter changes to the user's home directory.

mkdir [option(s)] directoryname

Generates a new directory.

rmdir [option(s)] directoryname

Erases the specified directory provided it is already void.

chown [option(s)] username.group file(s)

The ownership of a file can be transferred to the user with the specified user name.

-R

It changes files and directories in all sub-directories.

chgrp [option(s)] groupname file(s)

The group ownership of a given file can be transferred to the group with the specified group name.

chmod [options] mode file(s)

It changes the access permissions.

The mode parameter comprises of three parts: group, access, and access type. group accepts the following characters:

u

user

g

group

o

others

To gain access, the + symbol is used, and denied by the - symbol.

The access type is controlled by the following options:

r

read

w

write

x

execute — It helps execute files or change to the directory.

s

Set uid bit — the application or program is initiated as if it were initiated by the owner of the file.

gzip [parameters] file(s)

With the help of complex mathematical algorithms, this program is utilized to compress the contents of files. Files compressed in such a way are not meant to utilize as it is, they are first uncompressed, and then used. Compressed files, however, are given the extension .gz. **tar** command can be used to compress files.

-d

Decompresses the packed gzip files, and convert them to their original size so they can normally be processed (like the command **gunzip**).

tar options archive file(s)

The **tar** command is responsible for converting one file or usually several files into an archive. Compression is optional, and it depends on upon the user.

tar is a quite complex command as its options range is extremely wide. The most commonly used options are:

-f

Usually, the output is written on the screen, but this command writes the output to a file.

-c

Generates a new tar archive.

-r

It adds files to an existing archive.

-t

It outputs the contents of an archive.

-u

Adds files, but only those files that are newer than the files already present in the archive.

-x

Unpack files from an archive (*extraction*).

-z

Packs the resultant archive with **gzip.**

-j

Compresses the resultant archive with **bzip2.**

-v

It enlists the files processed.

The archive files produced by **tar** end with .tar. If the tar archive was also compressed using **gzip**, the ending is .tgz or .tar.gz. If it was compressed using **bzip2**, .tar.bz2.

locate pattern(s)

The locate command helps in finding the location of a specified file in the directory. Wild cards can be used to specify the file names if desired. The program is quick, as it does not have to search entire file system but can just use a database particularly created for the purpose. However, this advantage brings a drawback to the table, as locate command is unable to find any files produced after the recent update of its database. The database can be created by root with **updatedb.**

updatedb [options(s)]

This command implements an update of the database used by locate. If you want to include files in all the existing directories, run the program as root. It also makes sense to place it in the background by appending an ampersand (&), so you can instantly carry on working on the same command line (**updatedb &**).

find [option(s)]

If you want to search a particular file in given directory, this command will help in achieving the goal. The first argument specifies the directory in which the search should begin. The option –name must be followed by a search string, and the user is free to include wild cards, if necessary. In contrast to locate command which utilizes a database, file command scans the actual directory.

Here are some of the Linux command lines references for some common operations that are tested on both Fedora and Ubuntu.

LINUX COMMANDS FOR CD:

To save the copy of data cdrom

gzip < /dev/cdrom > cdrom.iso.gz

To develop cdrom image for contents of dir

mkisofs -V LABEL -r dir | gzip > cdrom.iso.gz

To clear CDRW

wodim dev=/dev/cdrom blank=fast

To develop cdrom image at/dir/mnt for reading

mount -o loop cdrom.iso /mnt/dir

To rip audio tracks from CD for waving files that are present in dir

cdparanoia -B

To clear cdrom image

wodim dev=/dev/cdrom blank=fast

To make audio CD through all wavs in present dir

wodim -v dev=/dev/cdrom -audio -pad *.wav

To develop ogg file from wav file

oggenc --tracknum=$track track.cdda.wav -o track.ogg

LINUX COMMANDS FOR DISK SPACE

To display files size big to small

ls -lSr

To segregate paths through simple to interpret disk usage

du -hs /home/* | sort -k1,1h

To display top disk users in present dir and also dutop

du -s * | sort -k1,1rn | head

To display free space on mounted file systems

df -h

To display free inodes over mounted file systems

df -i

To display disk partitions by types and sizes

fdisk -l

To prepare list of all packages through installed size (Kbytes) on deb distros

dpkg-query -W -f='${Installed-Size;10}\t${Package}\n' | sort -k1,1n

To prepare list of all packages through installed size (Bytes) over rpm distros

rpm -q -a --qf '%10{SIZE}\t%{NAME}\n' | sort -k1,1n

To develop large test file with no spacing

dd bs=1 seek=2TB if=/dev/null of=ext3.test

To shorten data of file or to develop an empty file

> file

LINUX COMMANDS FOR MONITORING OR DEBUGGING

To scrutinize messages on a log file

tail -f /var/log/messages

To sum up, profile system calls through command

strace -c ls >/dev/null

To note, system calls made through command

strace -f -e open ls >/dev/null

To scrutinize what is written to stdout and
stderr

strace -f -e trace=write -e write=1,2 ls >/dev/null

To list paths which process id that has open

lsof -p $$

To list procedures which have specified open path

lsof ~

To list, library calls made through command

ltrace -f -e getenv ls >/dev/null

To display network traffic apart from ssh

tcpdump not port 22

To list procedures through % cpu usage

ps -e -o pcpu,cpu,nice,state,cputime,args --sort pcpu | sed '/^ 0.0 /d'

To list procedures in hierarchy

ps -e -o pid,args --forest

To list procedures through mem (KB) usage

ps -e -orss=,args= | sort -b -k1,1n | pr -TW$COLUMNS

To list elapsed wall time for specific process IDs

ps -p 1,$$ -o etime=

To list all threads for specific processes

ps -C firefox-bin -L -o pid,tid,pcpu,state

To display system reboot history

last reboot

To show a changing process subtree

watch -n.1 pstree -Uacp $$

To display amount of remaining RAM

free -m

To monitor udev events to assists configure rules

udevadm monitor

To watch changeable data constantly

watch -n.1 'cat /proc/interrupts'

LINUX COMMANDS FOR SYSTEM INFORMATION

To display kernel version and system architecture

uname -a

To display all partitions registered on the system

cat /proc/partitions

To display version and name of distribution

head -n1 /etc/issue

To display, total RAM seen through the system

grep MemTotal /proc/meminfo

To display information on CPUs

grep "model name" /proc/cpuinfo

To display information on USB

lsusb -tv

To display information on PCI

lspci -tv

To list mounted file systems on the system and align output

mount | column -t

To show information on SMBIOS/DMI

dmidecode -q | less

To carry out a read speed test over disk sda

hdparm -tT /dev/sda

To display information on disk sda

hdparm -i /dev/sda

To know how long this disk or system has been powered in total

smartctl -A /dev/sda | grep Power_On_Hours

To test unreadable blocks on disk sda

badblocks -s /dev/sda

To display state of cells in laptop battery

grep -F capacity: /proc/acpi/battery/BAT0/info

LINUX COMMANDS FOR INTERACTIVE AND KEYBOARD SHORTCUTS

Line editor used by bash, python, bc, gnuplot

readline

Powerful file manager that can browse rpm, tar, ftp, ssh

mc

Virtual terminals with detaching capability

screen

Web browser

links

Interactive/scriptable graphing

gnuplot

open a file or url with the registered desktop application

xdg-open

LINUX COMMANDS FOR CALENDAR

To show a calendar

cal -3

To show calendar for specific month of the year

cal 9 1752

To exit a script except it is month's last day

[$(date -d '12:00 today +1 day' +%d) = '01'] || exit

To know what is the date on this Friday

date -d fri

To know what day Christmas falls in this year

date --date='25 Dec' +%A

To know what is the time in the west cost of United States

TZ='America/Los_Angeles' date

To know what is the local time for 9 am next Friday on west coast

date --date='TZ="America/Los_Angeles" 09:00 next Fri'

To convert seconds since the epoch to date

date --date='@2147483647'

LINUX COMMANDS FOR LOCALES

To print numbers with thousands assembling appropriate to locale

printf "%'d\n" 1234

To get information from locale database

echo "I live in `locale territory`"

To utilize locale thousands grouping in ls

BLOCK_SIZE=\'1 ls -l

To list fields available in locale database

locale -kc $(locale | sed -n 's/\(LC_.\{4,\}\)=.*/\1/p') | less

To check locale information for particular country

LANG=en_IE.utf8 locale int_prefix

LINUX COMMANDS FOR RECODE (OBSOLETES ICONV, DOS2UNIX, UNIX2DOS)

To display available conversions (aliases on every line)

recode -l | less

To convert Windows utf8 to local charset

recode utf-8/CRLF.. file_to_change.txt

To convert Windows "ansi" to local charset where auto does CRLF conversions recode windows-1252.. file_to_change.txt

To convert Latin9 (western europe) to utf8

recode iso-8859-15..utf8 file_to_change.txt

Quoted printable decode

recode /qp.. < file.qp > file.txt

Base64 encode

recode ../b64 < file.txt > file.b84

To convert text to HTML

recode ..HTML < file.txt > file.html

To check table of characters

recode -lf windows-1252 | grep euro

To display latin-9 encoding

echo -n 0x20AC | recode ucs-2/x2..latin-9/x

To display what a code represents in latin-9 charmap

echo -n 0x80 | recode latin-9/x1..dump

To display utf-8 encoding

echo -n 0x20AC | recode ucs-2/x2..utf-8/x

LINUX COMMANDS FOR MATH

For quick math

echo '(1 + sqrt(5))/2' | bc -l

To calculate π the unix way

seq -f '4/%g' 1 2 99999 | paste -sd-+ | bc -l

For Python handles scientific notation

echo 'pad=20; min=64; print (100E6)/((pad+min)*8)' | python

For More complex (int), for example This shows max FastE packet rate

echo 'pad=20; min=64; (100*10^6)/((pad+min)*8)' | bc

To plot FastE packet rate vs packet size

echo 'pad=20; plot [64:1518] (100*10**6)/((pad+x)*8)' | gnuplot -persist

For base conversion (hex to dec) ((shell arithmetic expansion))

echo $((0x2dec))

For base conversion that is decimal to hexadecimal

echo 'obase=16; ibase=10; 64206' | bc

du -hs /home/* | sort -k1,1h

LINUX COMMANDS FOR DIR NAVIGATION

Go to the previous dir

cd -

Go to dir, execute command and return to the current dir

cd dir && command)

Go to the $HOME dir

cd

Put the current dir on stack so that you can popd back to it

pushd .

LINUX COMMANDS FOR FILE SEARCH

Quick dir listing

alias l='ls -l --color=auto'

Print in 9 columns to width of the terminal

ls /usr/bin | pr -T9 -W$COLUMNS

Look for all the regular files for 'example' in this dir and below

find -type f -print0 | xargs -r0 grep -F 'example'

Process every item with multiple commands (in while loop)

find -maxdepth 1 -type d | while read dir; do echo $dir; echo cmd2; done

Locate directories not accessible by all (useful for website)

find -type d ! -perm -111

Locate files not readable by all (useful for website)

find -type f ! -perm -444

To look for the cached index for all names. This re is like glob *file*.txt

locate -r 'file[^/]*\.txt'

Fast sorted search dictionary for prefix

look reference

List all the files by date

ls -lrt

Find 'expr' in this dir and below

find -name '*.[ch]' | xargs grep -E 'expr'

Find all regular files for 'example' in this dir

find -maxdepth 1 -type f | xargs grep -F 'example'

LINUX COMMANDS FOR ARCHIVES AND COMPRESSION

To Encrypt a file

gpg -c file

To decrypt a file

gpg file.gpg

To backup harddisk to the remote machine

dd bs=1M if=/dev/sda | gzip | ssh user@remote 'dd of=sda.gz'

Creating compressed archive of dir

tar -c dir/ | bzip2 > dir.tar.bz2

Extracting an archive (use gzip and not bzip2 for tar.gz files)

bzip2 -dc dir.tar.bz2 | tar -x

Copy with permissions copy or dir to remote:/where/to/ dir

(tar -c /dir/to/copy) | ssh -C user@remote 'cd /where/to/ && tar -x -p'

Create an encrypted archive of dir/ on the remote machine

tar -c dir/ | gzip | gpg -c | ssh user@remote 'dd of=dir.tar.gz.gpg'

Copy with permissions the contents of copy or dir to /where/to/

(cd /dir/to/copy && tar -c .) | (cd /where/to/ && tar -x -p)

Create an archive of the subset of dir/ and below

find dir/ -name '*.txt' | tar -c --files-from=- | bzip2 > dir_txt.tar.bz2

Copy with permissions the copy or dir to /where/to/ dir

(tar -c /dir/to/copy) | (cd /where/to/ && tar -x -p)

Create an archive of the subset of dir/ and below

find dir/ -name '*.txt' | tar -c --files-from=- | bzip2 > dir_txt.tar.bz2

LINUX COMMAND FOR RSYNC

Get diffs only. Carry out number of times for troublesome downloads

rsync -P rsync://rsync.server.com/path/to/file file

Sync the current directory with the remote directory

rsync -auz -e ssh remote:/dir/ . && rsync -auz -e ssh . remote:/dir/

Copy with the rate limit. It is like nice for I and O

rsync --bwlimit=1000 fromfile tofile

Same website with using compression as well as encryption

rsync -az -e ssh --delete ~/public_html/ remote.com:'~/public_html'

LINUX COMMANDS FOR SECURE SHELL (ssh)

To run the command on $HOST as $USER. The default command will be shell

ssh $USER@$HOST command

To set up the public key for $USER@$HOST for the password-less log in

ssh-copy-id $USER@$HOST

To run the Ghrapical User Interface command on $HOSTNAME as $USER

ssh -f -Y $USER@$HOSTNAME xeyes

To promote the connections from $HOST:1434 to imap:143

ssh -R 1434:imap:143 root@$HOST

To duplicate with the permissions to $USER's home directory on $HOST

scp -p -r $USER@$HOST: file dir/

To promote the connections to $HOSTNAME:8080 out to $HOST:80

ssh -g -L 8080:localhost:80 root@$HOST

Use quicker crypto for local LAN

scp -c arcfour $USER@$LANHOST: bigfile

LINUX COMMANDS FOR WGET

Store up the local brows able version of page to current dir

(cd dir/ && wget -nd -pHEKk
http://www.pixelbeat.org/cmdline.html)

Professionally update the local copy of the web site

wget --mirror http://www.example.com/

Carry on the download of a partly downloaded file

wget -c http://www.example.com/large.file

Verify all the links in file

wget -nv --spider --force-html -i bookmarks.html

Downloading some files to existing directory

wget -r -nd -np -l1 -A '*.jpg' http://www.example.com/dir/

Do limited download (20KB/s)

wget --limit-rate=20k url

FTP maintains globbing

wget ftp://remote/file[1-9].iso/

Download the url at 1 AM to the existing dir

echo 'wget url' | at 01:00

Process the output straight

wget -q -O- http://www.pixelbeat.org/timeline.html | grep 'a href' | head

LINUX COMMANDS FOR NETWORKING

Display the status of the ethernet interface eth0

ethtool eth0

Search for whose information for the hostname or ip address

whois pixelbeat.org

Physically set the speed of ethernet interface

ethtool --change eth0 autoneg off speed 100 duplex full

Search for the local ip address (same as the host `hostname`)

hostname -i

Display the link status of the wireless interface wlan0

iw dev wlan0 link

Search for the DNS ip address for name/ vice versa

host pixelbeat.org

Physically set the speed of the wireless interface

iw dev wlan0 scan

List down the active connections to and from system

ss -tup

List down the wireless networks that are in range

iw dev wlan0 scan

List down all the internet services on system

ss -tupl

List down all the network interfaces

ip link show

Set the default gateway to 1.2.3.254

ip route adds default via 1.2.3.254

Rename the interface from eth0 to wan

ip link set dev eth0 name wan

List the routing table

ip route show

LINUX COMMANDS FOR WINDOWS NETWORKING

Search the Windows machine

smbtree

Send popup to the windows machine

echo 'message' | smbclient -M windows_box

Search forthe windows name that is associated with the ip address

nmblookup -A 1.2.3.4

Mount windows share

mount -t smbfs -o fmask=666,guest //windows_box/share /mnt/share

List the shares on samba server/windows machine

smbclient -L windows_box

LINUX COMMANDS FOR TEXT MANIPULATION

Changing string1 with string2

sed 's/string1/string2/g'

Combine and then separate line items to single line

```
seq 10 | paste -s -d ' '
```

Change anystring1 to anystring2

```
sed 's/\(.*\)1/\12/g'
```

Calculate lines

```
history | wc -l
```

Take out the comments as well as blank lines

```
sed '/^ *#/d; /^ *$/d'
```

Sort out non-printable characters

```
tr -dc '[:print:]' < /dev/urandom
```

Escape the shell metacharacters active within double quotes

```
sed 's/\([`"$\]\)/\\\1/g'
```

Conversion of case

```
echo 'Test' | tr '[:lower:]' '[:upper:]'
```

Align numbers accurately

```
seq 10 | sed "s/^/ /; s/ *\(.\{7,\}\)/\1/"
```

FindIPV4 ip addresses

```
sort -t. -k1,1n -k2,2n -k3,3n -k4,4n
```

Copying a column

```
seq 10 | sed p | paste - -
```

Remove a line

```
sed -i 42d ~/.ssh/known_hosts
```

Print thousandth line

sed -n '1000{p;q}'

Print the lines from 10 to 20

sed -n '10,20p;20q'

LINUX COMMANDS FOR SET OEPRATIONS

Merger of unsorted files

sort file1 file2 | uniq

Symmetric dissimilarity of the sorted files

join -t'\0' -v1 -v2 file1 file2

Connection of the unsorted files

sort file1 file2 | uniq -d

Dissimilarity of sorted files

join -t'\0' -v2 file1 file2

Dissimilarity of unsorted files

sort file1 file1 file2 | uniq -u

Combination of the sorted files

join -t'\0' -a1 -a2 file1 file2

Chapter 7: Linux Backup Techniques

Accidents can happen anytime without any warning bells. So, it is extremely important to have a safe place to store the data with the use of other hosts, tapes, floppy disks as well as CDs.

A reliable backup tool is something that is certainly not optional, and everyone should have one. This definitely does not imply that you need to spend a whole fortune on the backup to get a setup. A backup expense is one thing that you need to keep ready because you never know when the need will arise.

The administrative duties are not accomplished without backup operations, as they are an integral part of the administrative functions. The traditional dump/restore tools help you refine your backup process, as they detect data changes since the last backup.

Computer software utility, tar, helps in backing up and restoring particular files and directories in the form of archives. For backup purposes, tar is usually utilized with a tape device. The backups can be scheduled automatically by scheduling the suitable tar commands with the cron utility. You can also compress the archives to save the storage space. The compressed archive material can thus be extracted from the system to any medium, such as floppy disk, tape, or a DVD. However, while working on GNOME, you can utilize the option of File Roller to create archive files readily. In contrast, the KDAT tool on KDE back up archives to tapes which are believed as a front end to tar tool.

There are a number of solutions available in the market. A few are cost effective and have minimal features; others are expensive and full of features. There are several backup solutions available for the Linux operating system, and some popular and effective ones are mentioned below:

- Bacula

- Fwbackups

- Mondorescue
- Rsync
- Amanda
- Simple backup solution
- Back in time
- Box backup
- Arkeia
- Kbackup
- Areca backup
- Afbackup
- Tar
- Dump
- Cedar backup
- Duplicity
- Rsnapshot
- PING
- Partimage
- Clonezilla
- Zmanda
- Timevault
- Flyback

- AMANDA

Below are some pointers that you need to know regarding the Linux backup techniques:

- Create, question and the unpack the file archives

- Make Java archives

- Encrypt your important data

- Write a CD

- Look for important data to use the other backup

When choosing a backup for the Linux operating system, it is important for you to look for things such as auto-changers, backup media, open source software, data format, cross-platform support, volume shadow copy, reports and alerts, commercial support, deduplication, backup span multiple volumes, encryption data stream, etc.

Choosing the Right Backup Tool

The problem of choosing the right backup option is an important one. There are many options available. You should be able to find the one which works best for your needs. To help you choose, we will have a look at some popular backup options along with their pros and cons.

Amanda

The Advanced Maryland Automatic Network Disk Archiver, or simply Amanda is an open source product which can be acquired for free. It works best for moderately sized computer centers. It tapes drives, changers, and disks over a network and provides backing for multiple devices over that network.

Amanda uses a combination of master backup server and Unix or Windows. It can help you back up almost anything on a uniform network. LVM snapshots and hardware snapshots can be handled using this software. The master server manages the resources and ensures that the space and time required to backup anything are available.

The cons would include the centralization of the Amanda backup system. If your backup requirement does not include tapes or media, Amanda is not the right choice as it includes continuous filling up and changing; besides you would have to rely on a central server to manage everything. It is better to opt for a simpler solution as your needs may overkill Amanda. If your work requires media and a central system, you will really find Amanda the best option with its efficient backup and the ability to write tape and disk at the same time.

Bacula

Bacula is considered a good alternative to Amanda, but again it depends on your requirement. Like Amanda, Bacula is an open source and free to use. In order to use Bacula, you have to install client programs on every machine you want the backup for. It is controlled through a central server. Bacula uses its own file format instead of standard Unix tools for backup.

When you're using more than one server with different tape drives, Bacula is a better alternative as it does incremental and full routine backups. Encryption and RAIT are supported by Amanda whereas Bacula has a scripting language for customization. You can seek help from this language to create encryptions.

While deciding which of these two backup systems would work best, it comes down to your requirements and architecture. The preference of your staff should also be taken into consideration. If you're using a central backup server with one tape drive, Amanda will work best for you, and if you're using tape drives that are distributed across the network, Bacula would be the right pick.

BackupPC

BackupPC is designed for backing up Linux or WinXX laptops and desktops to a file server; it is also a free and open source. It is known for its high performance. It is being used at smaller scale operations efficiently.

The features offered include the ability to store and keep snapshots of a small company's desktop for a long period of time. Users can restore their own backups, the presence and absence of a particular computer (roaming laptop) can be detected. Reminders are given automatically in case you haven't backed up in sometime.

The web interface available to the user and the administrator can be used to initiate backups. Every file is stored in a specified and individual archive which allows an ease of access and quick recovery of both single files and a group.

The downsides of using BackupPC is its slow performance while doing large restores. It is also not a viable option for remote use in case you have a lot of data. The archives which you have compressed can only be read by tools of BackupPC which makes you completely reliant. The positive side is that being an open source, you can always keep the source code so that you have continuous access to the program.

Rsync

Different Linux backup solutions have rsync at the back end. It is a good tool which can be used in combination with scripting to make remote mirrors and other backup schemes. People who don't think they need a special backup tool personally or commercially will prefer this method.

Rsync can be run as a server daemo. It will give access to remote users to sync file copies to your system while keeping the entire directories and only transferring the changed files. You can update files without downloading the full version as mirror and software FTP sites which act as rsync servers.

Rsync can be used to remote-copy files or a directory from one host to another, making an intelligent and specific backup. Rsync is designed to copy only those files have been tweaked instead of the whole directory. The archive mode saves the ownership and permissions, giving the relevant users access through the host system.

The simple setup of this tool makes it a good choice while doing an impromptu backup. Rsync works best when you need more backup in the form of duplication (this can include copying the files, directories, and website content to a different site).

Commercial Linux backup products

Symantec Corp.'s Vertias NetBackup Enterprise is a good option if you're looking for commercial Linux backup product. It is an enterprise-level server that provides support for Windows, many Unix flavors, and Linux. It also offers special support to various virtual environments like VMware.

NetBackup maintains a dashboard which provides insight into capacity, the trends, the charges and costs of recovery and backup services, compliance and more. This is the best option for you if you don't want to maintain your own reporting or find other solutions you're using unsatisfactory.

Symantec's Backup Exec along with Linux agent and BakBone Software's NetVault are other popular commercial backup solutions.

Having a solid backup and recovery plan is a must when you're looking for a Linux backup tool. The solution doesn't work until you've tested your ability to restore data. You have to look at it in the bigger picture when choosing the backup software. This will ensure that you're protected, in the real sense.

Chapter 8: Setting Up a Linux Printer

One of the few pieces of hardware that lead to trouble with the Linux system is the printer. However, it is simple to check to see if your printer is supported or not. Once you know that the printer is supported, it will take only a few steps to get it work for you.

There are a few very rare cases where you will find that the printer is not marked as functional, however, to be on the safer side it is good to stick to the general rule, and that is to check the compatibility.

In order to check if your printer is supported or not, you can make use of OpenPrinting Database and search for your printer. With this, you can get an idea whether the printer is known to work entirely or partially.

You can do this with your current printer. However, it will only give you an idea of how well the printer will work on Linux. This database can prove to be useful for you when you are searching for the new printer. On the basis of that, you can check out the models that work on Linux.

Once you have the printer that the database says will work with Linux, you have three possible options available for getting it started. The three options available are plug and play, install a package from your distribution repositories, and get the driver from the manufacturer's website.

At times, the printer will work as soon as you plug it in. This is possible because the driver is already in the Linux Kernel or it can be due to the fact that the package that you would require is installed by default in your distribution. In case it does not work, then you will be required to install the package from your distribution repositories.

At the time the printer is added to the printer configuration window, it should identify that the printer is attached and will automatically check out the package that comprises the needed driver.

Printer Installation - Explained

All the Linux systems depend on a user-friendly printer configuration tool known as system-config-printer. There might be slight differences in GUI (depending on the distribution you have chosen), but the tool is used for the same purpose. A web front-end for the Common Unix Printing System (CUPS) makes the process of managing Linux printer extremely simple, even without the presence of GUI tool. Printers can be configured remotely using this effective tool.

We will now focus our attention on the process of installing printers for Linux using the system-config-printer tool. After reading through the steps, you'll realize that it was really simple, and you'd stop worrying about using Linux as a desktop or even using it to share the printers out.

Almost all the distribution has the tools to manage printers; you would not need to worry about installing it. The process of finding the tool is slightly different among different distributions like in Deepin; the dash-like menu has to be opened, and you would have to search for system section. You'll be able to find Printers within this section. You would just need to type 'printer' after opening Dash in Ubuntu. Then click on the printer tool to open system-config-printer. If you've already connected the printer to the desktop, and you don't find system-config-printer there, then you don't have to worry. It is unlikely that you won't find your printer there as Linux printer support has matured and almost all printers are supported. Anyways, you can add your printer by following this approach whether it is supported or not.

Adding Local Printers

Click on the Add button from the system-config-printer window. You can then select a listed printer to add from the resulting window. In case you don't see the printer listed, you would have to locate the drivers for that printer. Apart from the manufacturing website of the printers, you can find the drivers on Linux Foundation's OpenPrinting work group. The driver database is extensive on OpenPrinting. You can find your printer from the listings and then see the driver which is suggested by OpenPrinting.

After you've added the driver, start the process again and this time, when you click on Add button, you will be able to see your printer on the list. After you select your printer and click 'Forward', system-config-printer will present the Printer Description window after it has searched for the drivers.

The description should be made as simply as possible. It should be something which you should be able to understand easily. You can add 'printer' or 'laser printer' for the short name, model number in the description and location of the printer for location. After you've added the description, you can click on Apply to finish the process. You can click on Print Test Page if you like.

In order to make sure that other systems have access, you can right click the printer and see both the checkboxes 'Enabled' and 'Shared' are checked. In case they are not, you can click to enable them.

Adding Network Printers

The process of adding network printers is as simple as adding a local printer. It is natural that a hosting system will determine and dictate how the printer is added to the Linux system. Let's assume that the printer which is to be added is on another Linux system on LAN.

The initial step is again similar; you have to open the system-config printer tool. Now, click on Add and click 'Network Printer' to see more options in the expanded form. You will see two options here. Either the network printer is listed already in case it was already shared out, or the host is not listed.

If the hostname is already listed, you can click on it and then select the printer. Repeat the same process of clicking Forward, filling out the description for the printer and clicking apply. Your printer is now ready to be used.

In case the hostname doesn't appear in the network printer list, enter the IP address of the host system and then click on 'Find Network Printer'. Uniform Resource Indicator (URI) device will be automatically filled out; you will just need to click on 'Forward' and add the description for the printer. Just click 'Apply' after you are done adding the description and your printer will be accessible.

Printing with Linux has been made really easy. The only possible issue you might be facing would be an incorrect driver. The tools are mature and easy to use; the Linux hardware support has become a piece of cake.

Conclusion

I hope that the information you have learned from this book proved to be useful in helping you understand the potential of the Linux system and how you can use basic commands for day-to-day functions.

If you have been able to put at least one of the things you learned here to use, my purpose of creating this book is fulfilled.

This book will serve you well as the first step in learning about Linux. It is a very vast topic, and as you begin to use it, you will have more ideas, questions, and issues. There are numerous videos and online reference materials available to you, should you run into complex issues. I would strongly recommend readers keep this book handy on your computer and use as a reference for the future.

Made in the USA
Lexington, KY
21 February 2017